O9-BTJ-595

XF
LIN

Lindeen, Mary.
Tuesday

FRA

DATE DUE

Tuesday

by Mary Lindeen • illustrated by Javier González

Content Consultant: Susan Kesselring, M.A., Literacy Educator and Preschool Director

ST. MARY PARISH LIBRARY
FRANKLIN, LOUISIANA

magic wagon

visit us at
www.abdopublishing.com

Published by Magic Wagon, a division of the ABDO Publishing Group, 8000 West 78th Street, Edina, Minnesota,
55439. Copyright © 2008 by Abdo Consulting Group, Inc. International copyrights reserved in all countries. All rights
reserved. No part of this book may be reproduced in any form without written permission from the publisher.
Looking Glass Library™ is a trademark and logo of Magic Wagon.

Printed in the United States.

Text by Mary Lindeen
Illustrations by Javier González
Edited by Patricia Stockland
Interior layout and design by Becky Daum
Cover design by Becky Daum

Library of Congress Cataloging-in-Publication Data

Lindeen, Mary.
  Tuesday / Mary Lindeen ; illustrated by Javier A. González ; content consultant Susan Kesselring.
    p. cm. — (Days of the week)
  ISBN 978-1-60270-098-7
  I. Days—Juvenile literature. I. González, Javier A., 1974– ill. II. Kesselring, Susan. III. Title.
  GR930.L567 2008
  529'.1—dc22

                                    2007034064

The seven days in a week

are always the same.

First Sunday, then Monday,

what's the next one to name?

It's Tuesday! That's right.

Tuesday's day number three.

But how did that happen?

How can that be?

The day starts with a "two" sound.

Is it really the third?

Yes!

"Two" is not really part of the word.

On Tuesdays most often

it is the rule

that people must go

to work or to school.

Some Tuesdays are filled

with big holiday fun,

like Fat Tuesday, or Mardi Gras.

We love that one!

One Tuesday that's special
comes in the fall.
This Tuesday in November's
a big deal for all.

It is a day

that most grown-ups note.

On this very big Tuesday,

they line up and vote.

Tuesday's a great day

to play with your friends,

watch movies, or read books.

The fun never ends!

You did all your chores.

This Tuesday is done.

Tomorrow is Wednesday,

a new day for fun!

The Days of the Week

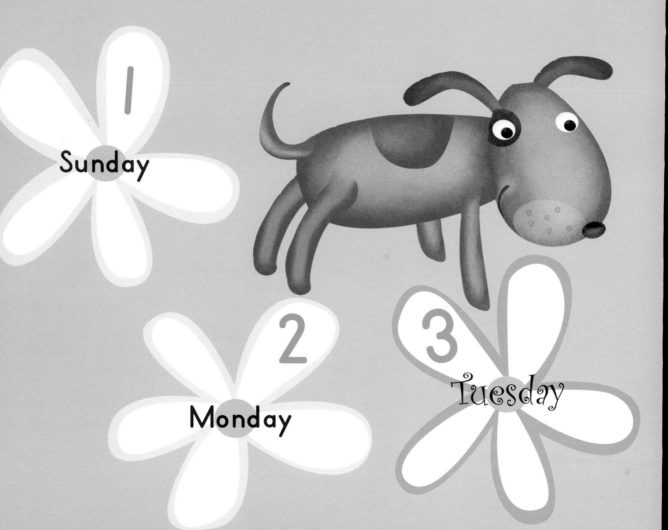

1 Sunday

2 Monday

3 Tuesday

7 Saturday

4 Wednesday

6 Friday

5 Thursday

A TUESDAY CELEBRATION

Have your own Mardi Gras parade. Dress up in fancy clothes and wear necklaces you've made by stringing dry pasta tubes on yarn. Then, parade around your classroom or your yard.

A THANK YOU FOR YOUR TEACHER

Make something special for your favorite teacher. Pick a bouquet of flowers from the garden, or draw a special picture. Then, give it to your favorite teacher on Tuesday, along with a great big "Thank you for all you do!"

READ A TUESDAY STORY

Did you know that Winnie the Pooh and his friends always do important things on Tuesdays? Piglet spends every Tuesday at Christopher Robin's house, and Kanga goes to Pooh's house every Tuesday to teach Pooh how to jump. Rabbit and Roo spend their Tuesdays together, too. On Tuesday, make time to read your favorite Winnie the Pooh story!

WORDS TO KNOW

chore: the daily work of a house or farm.

holiday: a special festival or celebration day, when people don't go to work or school as they usually would do.

Mardi Gras: a carnival, or party, held to celebrate feasting and Lent.

tomorrow: the day after today.

vote: to pick someone or something.